After Hours explores mortality and transience in the lives of Irish migrants that settled in England in the first half of the 20th century, and the generations that followed them. At the heart of this collection is an elegiac sequence of poems in memory of David Cooke's father-in-law, a larger than life Irishman who met illness and death with good-humoured resilience.

David Cooke was born in the UK in 1953 to a family that comes from the West of Ireland. He won a Gregory Award in 1977, while still an undergraduate at Nottingham University. After publishing his first full poetry collection in 1984, he then wrote no poetry for two decades, during which time he was Head of Modern Languages in a large comprehensive school in Cleethorpes. Subsequently, he earned his living as an online bookseller, but is now happily retired. He is married with four grown-up children.

Also by David Cooke

Brueghel's Dancers: Poems (Free Man's Press, 1984)
In the Distance (Night Publishing, 2011)
Work Horses (Ward Wood Publishing, 2012)
A Mumuration (Two Rivers Press, 2015)
A Slow Blues, New and Selected Poems (The High Window Press, 2015)

AFTER HOURS

David Cooke

Cultured Llama Publishing

First published in 2017 by
Cultured Llama Publishing
www.culturedllama.co.uk

The right of David Cooke to be identified as the
author of this work has been asserted by him
in accordance with Section 77 of the Copyright,
Designs and Patents Act 1988

A CIP record for this book is available from The British Library

ISBN 978-0-9957381-0-2

Printed in Great Britain by Lightning Source UK Ltd

Cover design: Mark Holihan
Cover photograph: Peadar O'Donoghue
Author photograph: Phyll Smith

In memory of John Durr
1931–2011

Omnia tempus habent,
et suis spatiis transeunt universa sub caelo

Ecclesiastes 3:1

Contents

Lineage

Devotee of high jinks
and a wry exponent
of strange logic,
he had always loved
the children –
his own at first
and then theirs
until, one by one
in the days
of his decline,
he saw them in –
a new generation
for whom
he would never
be more than a name.

FOR THE RECORD

Le Petit Parisien, 1952

A small boy running, but not for his life,
as all can see in his fearless smile
and the sense of freedom

that lights his eyes. This is the day
he will always remember,
important only because of an errand

and the small coin he didn't drop,
holding it up on tiptoes
across the counter of a baker's shop,

disregarding for once
the glass-fronted shelves of pastries
laid out on a lower level.

The still warm, unwieldy baguette
stowed beneath his arm,
he races homewards.

At his feet, his shadow,
foreshortened, inscrutable,
can only just keep up, one step behind.

Shape-shifting, a demon,
it seems momentarily a cat –
its back hunched, its dark pelt bristling.

My Grandson Writes His Name
for Ziyad

The first letter he has known for months
in zigzag lines getting nowhere.

Turned on its side and crayoned blue
he can stretch it out like a river;

or if he changes colour can make
a mountain, some grass, a fire.

Cut back to its simplest form
and laid out in rows like ghosts,

he follows the dots over and over
before he does it on his own.

When he learns its sound is a buzz
he likes, he hears it and sees it again

in the stripes of *zebra*,
in the bars of a place called *zoo*.

He has five shapes to master.
They stand above or hang below

a line that's always there –
even if you think it's vanished.

But when it all comes together
in a final downward stroke

– staunch and straight as he will be –
it tells him who he is,

this name he has always heard
ever since he's been here.

Scholars

Die Welt zerfällt in Tatsachen.
Ludwig Wittgenstein, *Tractatus Logico-Philosophicus*

In the high-ceilinged rooms
of ragged schools you hear
the clack of chalk on slates.

Heads down, still breathing,
they are figuring out,
applying the rules

they hope will get it straight.
The first day they dip
their pens into tiny china wells

the mistress smiles
and tells them
to call this their 'copy work'.

It is letters and words,
then sentences,
the bare bones of wisdom.

When the time has come
they will learn to think.
Meanwhile the neat

inherit the earth –
for if they smudge it
the page is spoiled.

Beyond high windows
the world exists.
It is made up of the facts

they are gathering one by one.
All day long they raise their hands,
owning up to their futures.

For the Record

Without so much as a thread of decency,
Antoninus Elagabalus, high priest
and mother's boy, made biographers weep.
Proponents of discipline almost choked,
repeating the syllables of his name.

His sculpted head is unremarkable
and bears no trace of his supposed excesses;
the muddled genes of his outlandishness
those of a handsome kid who, like the best
of us, will sometimes try it on.

In the fevered prose of his narration,
Lampridius got stuck in with dismay
and the fervour of a red-top hack.
As he took prim steps along the gutter,
he lamented earlier days.

Trawling the city's desolate quays
for the wayward and well-hung,
an inner circle supplied the emperor's needs,
while he, disguised as Venus,
mooned enticingly on the street.

When thugs who had raised him
had enough, they cut him down as swiftly
in a dank latrine, then turned towards Severus
who, 'after certain recent events',
was always bound to shine the brighter.

Chez Maxe, Joinville, 1947

With no finesse or finish, but still
a ladies' man, his steps are those
of a country dance or a dance
implying country matters.
No rise and fall, no pull through,
his frame dissolves in swagger
as he takes in hand his two girls
who, less impressed than he imagines,
are riding the waves of riffs and wails,
the imported sounds of freedom,
in a public space where they embrace
la vie en rose and where so recently
their sisters were stripped,
cropped, and smeared.

Aretha Franklin

Your father could hold a congregation
in the palms of his hands raised to heaven;
and when he spoke of Daniel
at prayer in the lion's den his words
were a song. His wayward daughter,
with your gift, like his, God-given,
were you a sinner or sinned against
the first time you weakened?

It takes you years to find an answer
and years to find a voice
beyond polished album tracks,
the smooth-talking lovers.
Laying down your own chords
at Muscle Shoals in Alabama,
you sang like a natural woman –
my listlessness dissolving in my rapt *Amen!*

Le Nu Provençal

She is like Eve in exile,
awakening each morning
when the sun has risen,
then rising herself,
shackled to the day's routine.

She opens a shutter,
and the light sweeps in
across the uneven stone floor –
her summons to the tasks
that lie before her.

But first a strip-wash,
the astringent purity
of her ablutions. Leaning over
a basin, the chill water
unseals her eyes.

Still only half awake,
she takes in the tarnished
mirror, a chair; and sees how little
is needed to live
on the far side of paradise.

Piano

As a child I had wanted to play it,
so made sure my own had lessons.
Forking out those straitened days
for a decent secondhand one,
we got the best we could.
Iron-framed, in tune, it slotted
neatly into the empty alcove.

To this day our eldest is a fan
of the classics and made
a good fist of the *Pathéthique*.
Using the basics he'd mastered,
his brother joined a band.
Too young, the twins clumped
through anthems of dissent.

Toward the end of my twenties
I'd signed up myself for lessons
with Kate. Ten in a group
of late starters, she brought to heel
our wayward notes. Showing us
scales, the broken chords,
it soon all made sense.

The last time we came together
the man who checked our names
told us the little he knew, that piano wire
was what she'd chosen; and later
when the kids left home
the piano grieved in silence.
It was all we could do to give it away.

The Lovers at the Bastille

By the time they have reached
their vantage point they know
for certain that this is the day,
fixed in their memory
as their image is fixed in mine.

Across the city's foundering
skyline, its chaos of roofs,
they see how in wintry light
Notre Dame is holding out
like an island under siege.

For a few moments longer
they'll stay, as one by one
beneath them shutters close
and the day's work ceases
in shops and *ateliers*.

Groomed for the afternoon
he has spent with her, he leans
over and whispers something
he has maybe said before –
some foolishness or a vow.

All we see of her is her back
in a tailored suit, her stance
and its hint of purpose. Knowing
the world for what it is,
she will seek her place in it.

Peggy

My aunt Peg was a country girl
who couldn't wait to leave it.
She was flighty, flirty,
and married a gambler
with a Clark Gable moustache.

The first place they took her on
was a Camden Town tea room
where they had a Margaret,
so made her a Peggy
instead, as if that day

were a new beginning
among the fancies,
scones, and slices –
the serviettes and doilies
she insisted upon

until the end of her days –
like the fags that kept her slim,
out of sight in a wardrobe
long after, officially,
she had 'packed them in'.

In the photo they placed
on the coffin she looks
like a Forties starlet. Her head
at an angle, she's staring
into a softer light.

Mill Girl

In the quietness between
before and after, the girl
unspools her broken thread,
addressing the problem
of time she has lost.

Abstracted, briefly,
from her routine,
her posture is that
of a handmaid or lover
bestowing an intimate gift.

Yet kneeling there,
on her own, she is like
an *ingénue*, taking in
some visitant's
otherworldly news.

Her arms stretched
before her, she seems
to play invisible strings,
a harp whose cadences fade
into the noise beyond her.

Photographer

That was the day your shutter
stopped time and when, unaware
of how you do it, you pulled it off again.

And *That was the day*
was all you'd say, drawing us in
to stories that mean nothing to us

or the girl on the overhead train
beyond the fact
of light's alchemy

and the way it makes her face
a mirror because she is looking
towards us

while others are turned away,
their shoulders bearing the weight
of mundane shadows.

On Their Blindness

1. Losing the Light
   Rilke

She sat amongst them drinking her tea.
I saw from the start something different
in the way she held her cup.
She smiled once. I found it unsettling;
and when, at length, they all stood up,
to make their way through various rooms,
laughing all the while, I watched her
following: like one about to make
her entrance and sing to a crowd.

In her eyes joy played like sunlight
on the surface of a pool. Trailing
behind them, she took her time,
as if an obstacle blocked her way,
which she would have to overcome
before, unsteadily, she rose on wings.

2. The Blind Man in the Studio
Seán Ó Riordáin

'Sit down and I'll draw you,'
I said to the blind man.
'There's a chair in the corner
near you.' Turning towards it,
he stretched out a hand
well used to finding its way.
Each finger stroking the air
as a harpist strokes the strings,
he played the notes of silence,
his own secret lament
until, like a tentative swimmer
who has reached the bank,
he caught hold of the chair
and eased down into it.
Next thing he's a ladies' man
adjusting his hair.

Flying a Kite in People's Park

The man and the boy are struggling
– as they will in the years ahead –
to set free their tangled bird.
With air and sky enough
to lift it, all they need is luck
and the right approach
to see it soar, to keep it anchored.

A FLORIDA MORNING

A Florida Morning

Going downstairs to set up our breakfast
in the late morning sunshine out on the patio,
we are spoiled by the choice of what we can eat –
the brightly packaged cereals, the pastries
we bake for ourselves from a tube of dough,
or chilled cubes of fragrant melon,
pale yellow or pink, mixed with a yoghurt
we carve from its tub with a spoon.

And laying down the day's foundation,
I drink my coffee, its dark warmth winding
through me when, on its sticks of legs,
I notice a heron stalking the edge
of the pond: all the way round
and back again without a scrap to eat
among the bobbing soda cans
and a long-abandoned, half-deflated ball.

Higher up on a rooftop the second bird
who, for all I know, has feasted well
elsewhere, strikes an ascetic pose –
as if to say sometimes it's good
to rise above your hunger and make a shape
against the sky, its raised beak
a calamus, poised to inscribe an abstract
word on some precious parchment.

The Morikami Gardens, Florida

When you have been there you will understand
how a garden can grow inside your head
as it grew once inside the mind of one
who planned it on recalcitrant acres,
cleared first by migrant farmers, their patience
tried by blighted crops and their lack of wives.

In the end their colony failed, leaving
behind its stubborn founder who soldiered on
and made his money like a home-grown Yank.
Pearl Harbour, Enola Gay: no gesture
rights such wrongs, but now the land he gifted
proclaims, at least, the healing power of art.

And through a window called the Wisdom Ring,
you will learn again the ways of seeing,
appraising through its lens the formal view
of an island and the placement of trees
against a theatrical arc of sky
whose light diffuses across still water.

Passing over the Memorial Bridge
you will sense how, at every turn, pathways
fulfilling their basic function have a part
to play in the trickery of delight,
concealing and revealing a hillside
that closer up becomes a boxwood hedge;

and then leading you on until you're duped
by an expanse of 'borrowed scenery'.
In this leisurely maze where every path
is a texture, a concept, a history,
there's nothing growing that wasn't chosen
and nothing natural that isn't tweaked.

Beyond the lake, the tallest trees have formed
a screen so composed it might be freshly
painted, as if it hadn't taken years
to earn its place in the original scheme,
while, close at hand, the ornamental growth
is checked and braced against bamboo and wire,

each delicate branch enhanced in benign
crucifixion; and here where all is shape
and balance the one thing you haven't missed
is colour until, in unexpected
blossom, you see through leafage purple flames
burning slowly on some totemic tree.

Yet once you've crossed the Paradise Garden,
beneath which memories of plague and strife
lie buried, you'll reach a sanctuary
where art is reduced to swirls of gravel
that set the mind free, and where one boulder
and a fern is what remains of the world.

Driving

For three weeks
in Boca Raton I lost
my sense of direction –
however often
they told me
that East was the Ocean
and West Inland
I couldn't quite
equate it
to left or right,
driving wrong-handedly
on roads
that stretched
all ways before me
as far as the eye
could see.

And checking up
on the cars behind
I saw how
in the rear-view mirror
a compass point
lit up, showing
the way ahead –
which might
have been some use
if I'd had
a bigger picture
beyond
that endless grid
of featureless
gated communities
and interchangeable malls.

Fort Lauderdale

All around the harbour, its sprawling map
of islands in what was once a mangrove swamp
makes little sense to us whose eyes
are drawn to palm-occluded channels

and where, off limits, we merely gawp
from our cocky tourist launch at ostentatious
privacy. It might be Venice stripped
of history before the rot sets in,

an absentees' playground where, once
or twice a year, a movie star, a garbage man,
or a junk food mogul, touches base
and makes the most of a sky he's paid for.

And how inert the quietness
of those mausoleums whose phantom staff
maintain and watch high-tech interiors,
the sprinklered lawns, where sculpted herons

or wall-eyed, ironic gators,
are all that's left of chaos. Chugging past
the ramparts of each ocean-going yacht,
their iridescent blues and greys, a blaze of white,

we head for open seas, then turn about,
alerted to the presence of a solitary
manatee, whose indolent form eludes me,
however hard I look across the shifting water.

Loxahatchee

When I said *Loxahatchee*
to Taras, our Russian neighbour,
he said *Well, you know*
it isn't a park, it's only Nature –
as if by flagging
its lack of amenities
he'd spare me a pointless drive,
when Nature, really,
was all I wanted,
caged in as I was between
Palmetto and Glades,
locked down
by Lyons and Dixie –
imagining flocks
of startled waders
storming the heavens
in flittering clouds;
or a snail kite tracing
its casual orbits
above lost miles
of sawgrass swamp;
and *Loxahatchee*
was a tribal song
whose twisted roots
went deep into the dark
regenerative mud
where all things
had their beginning
and where in the end
they may return.

Ornithology

Here, where no one seems to walk,
they couldn't give the name of a bird
whose loosely gathered congregation
sweeps the mild midwinter sky
between Miami and Boca.

And so I noted down the details
to help me find it later: the lightly
coloured head it's hard to see
beyond its dark expansive
wings, the blunt edge of its tail.

The one time I saw them grounded
I sensed how even they were anchored
to necessity, their trailing wings
the robes of Rembrandt scholars
around some broken thing;

and stripping out its sinews
in a clueless, botched dissection,
they had their fill and rose again
into the swirl of the air
like charred scraps above a bonfire.

Bamboo
for Helen

The overarching bamboo grove
in the Morikami Gardens is nothing
more than grass writ large,
or grass the way we'd see it,
if we were tiny creatures.

In the wet heat of Florida
it grows four feet a day.
With its hollow, knuckled stems,
packed with strength and music,
it has a thousand uses –

from workaday tables
and chairs to screens
or the playful *shishi odoshi*
that scatters skittering deer
from a new plantation,

its equilibrium stirred
by silver chains of water
until, with a resonant
poc! the final pipe
has struck an oblate stone.

And when the breeze is rising,
the bamboo grove becomes
a fleet creaking slowly homewards,
even though its masts
are rooted in a foreign soil.

AFTER HOURS

Last Orders

The first thing we had to clear was the one
he prized the most: the cluttered pinewood bar
he'd salvaged from a neighbour moving on
at the end of the nineteen seventies.

Embalmed in a gloopy coat of varnish
that set to a brittle sheen, it lacked retro chic,
scuffed down to the wood along its edges,
its surface crazed with memories.

In the days when family came to stay
it placed him centre stage, measuring out
precisely his perfect Irish coffees
or each medicinal dose of whiskey.

And yet, for all its high stool bonhomie,
we dumped it, an eyesore for the viewers –
then missed a convenient shelf, sorting mail
that even now in his posthumous life

makes him offers he can't refuse.
Behind it was a glory hole that clanked
to the music of jumbled glasses
and the unopened bottles of 'quare stuff'

brought back from their hols by others –
when his own preference was Jameson's,
Paddy's, or the rank *poitín* he cracked open
in a conspiratorial hush.

Redundancy

The happiest days of his life were those
they paid him for doing nothing.
Selling up in the south, he moved north

to a cheap resort, where he had
all the time in the world
for setting the world to rights.

Walking and talking to strangers,
forever mooching about, he ambushed
all who listened, forced now

to state their opinions on bees
that buzzed in his bonnet –
his commissarial Soviet hat,

picked up for the *craic*
in a Sunday Market when the empire
fell – like the Brits' before it.

An unregenerate union man,
forged in the foundry at Ford's,
shaky hands compelled him to drudge,

unfit for trickier tasks;
but didn't stop him raking shares
in utilities Thatcher sold.

Along the beach his dog lopes on,
as he quizzes again, as if
for the first time, stooped figures

hunting for bait. 'They were digging
for *werms*', he will tell us later,
but not before he explains to them

why his dog's called *Red* –
not for its pelt or his politics,
but short for the deal that freed him.

Chemo

The six months they gave you and which,
in no time, became a year
are stretching out into another.

It seems that minutes and hours
are made of stubborn stuff. They are filled
with nonsense that keeps you going –

your repertoire of dud jokes
or the crazy hat you wore all winter
to show the world you hadn't gone.

The chemo chases through your system,
erupting here and there: your blistered throat
so raw it quietens you for days;

the scurf that scalds
your face. You have shucked off
loosened toenails

and hold out your fingertips.
They are blank, abraded. You claim defiantly
that now the cops can't trace you.

Routines

The simplest routines can save us: the phone call
a daughter makes each morning at nine o'clock
in which the words are nothing but tokens
worn to a sliver, or small change so valueless
you'd wonder why it's minted.
                              But then,
like nothing else, the routine alerts us
when the call's unanswered and we try again,
and then once more, knowing the silence
can be explained by a short walk
to the paper shop, or a problem with his stoma
that stops him picking up, while just in case
we cross town through fixated traffic
to where he's beached on soiled sheets,
hapless and alone.
                    Through a night
of whispering, of resignation and last rites,
his daughter keeps her vigil
until he blinks and then returns,
from wherever, alive at his own wake,
flirting outrageously with his nurses,
and wondering slyly if by chance
he'd be OK for a Guinness.

The Home

Purpose-built for final days
and all that they entail
of good, bad, indifferent,
it lies at the end of a block drive,
power-hosed and sealed against
the encroachment of weeds.

With its mock-Tudor fascia
of black painted beams,
criss-crossed and dependable,
it looms up to greet us
with unflappable cheeriness,
its brickwork proof

against the years' attrition.
It's there I see you still, resolute
and cranky, your good humour
seeping away, a clouded ichor,
as nonetheless, falteringly,
you raise yourself from a chair.

Gripping a frame that gives
you backbone, you take small
steps along the corridor,
unaware, as you concentrate,
of the bed-bound frailty of others
whose doors are always ajar.

Returning to your own,
you see through the window
horses in a paddock,
but then catch, excitedly, the glint
of foxes which we, too, make out
just before they vanish.

Whiskey

Your eightieth birthday came and went –
the landmark it seemed important to reach
in the last days of independence
before you quit the house.

On a street where you'd lived
for twenty years, refusing stubbornly
to lock a door, your English neighbours
brought you whiskey –
Irish, of course, and spelled
with an 'e', except for the orphaned
bottle of scotch we knew
you'd view askance.

Week by week in the home you worked
through them, one ritual tot a day.
Down at last to a rogue bottle,
I decanted it carefully
into the empty of Jameson –
a triumph, I thought, of form over substance.

31 Garnett Street

It had always been a smart move
to relocate to Cleethorpes where,
down-at-heel and windswept,
its unassuming streets found time
to indulge a 'character'
whose lilting and incorrigible
gift of the gab was all
he needed to keep him happy.

Cute enough in his own way,
or perhaps just lucky, he sold up
in a bubble we never dreamt
would burst, and then
cashed in, a thrifty Midas,
on the north-south divide
with a crock of gold
he scarcely ever touched.

And now he's gone, he leaves
behind a house that's hard
to shift, a theoretical asset
that each month will seem
more trouble than it's worth
in long-distance fractious
pow-wows over a few last sticks,
or the lick of paint no one's up for.

Effects

So this in the end is what it comes to,
the junk that remains when the best
is all picked over: his shamrock kitsch,
old souvenirs, his family name
inscribed on a framed parchment.

From the bay window we've cleared
'rustic' pottery we bought for ourselves
in our nesting phase, but then passed on,
unused, when they first moved in.

With anything else that's saleable
we'll box it for charity.
Whatever isn't will go in a bin –
like the binoculars I fancied keeping
but couldn't get to focus,
even when like a fool I noticed
I hadn't removed
the caps from the lenses.

French Park

How many days of emptiness,
endured and then unnoticed,
before estrangement settles in
like unchanging weather?

On soft mornings your mother rises,
the stationmaster's English wife,
no longer even mindful
of how good looks and blarney

brought her to this pass –
with all her talents on the shelf
too fine to be of use
and two small children suddenly

more than she can handle.
She will write you letters
you will not see. The hired help
will ruin you. In time

our secrets bleed through
the myths in which we bind them.
Towards the end you'll learn
you never were abandoned

and how behind locked doors,
querulous and lucid, she raged
at each request denied
by unsmiling, veiled bitches.

Going Home

Stage Irish, for sure, and patriotic
to a fault, you were self-styled *Irish John*,
defining yourself by allegiance
to a place that doesn't exist
beyond exiled memories.

Through intransigent years
of bomb blasts, reprisals,
you picked over endlessly
the bleak bones of history
with me goading you to tell me

why you never returned,
knowing contentiousness
was your delight, the devilment
in a schoolboy who winked each time
they caned him. Fearless to the end,

you were ready to go,
and so I'll say goodbye,
trying now to get it right –
how one who leaves says *slán agat!*
and one who remains *slán leat!*

After Hours

1. An Electric Chair

Now and then she stares
at the window, wondering
where he's skulked off to.

She has a remote
to change the channel and one
that has raised her feet.

2. Talents

All her talents slipped
away. We ditch her paintings,
her ancient Singer.

3. Man and Wife

Whatever he did,
it never seemed to please her,
though God knows for years

he had tried his best.
Her glass was always empty.
His was mostly full.

4. Saturday

First it's evening Mass
and then he's off to his club:
a sociable gent.

5. Fathers

If mine had survived
they might have had some sessions,
the union man,

the ganger, their red
and blue dissolving somehow
into shades of green.

6. A Quiet Pint

Our pints of Guinness
look like priests. Eyeing them up,
we drink them slowly.

7. Laid Out

He has scrubbed up well.
His daughter pins his relic
onto his lapel.

There's holy water
sent from Knock, the set of beads
his cold hands fumbled.

8. Funeral parlour

So many people
in a small space. There are some
whose eyes do not meet.

9. Poem

I read the poem
I wrote for him, the only
one he ever saw.

Now those he'll never
know can make his acquaintance,
if I've got him right.

10. Oration

With *beannacht Dé leat*
and *slán abhaile* it's time
to call it a day.

11. Cortege

The requiem Mass
over, our streeling convoy
heads toward the crem.

I've turned too early –
those behind follow me up
and back down again.

12. Flowers

He would have loved this
tricolour spray: white roses,
leaves, chrysanthemums.

13. The Dresser

The repro dresser
is heaving with all the bumf
her father left her.

Whatever she needs
is always buried until
she resurrects it.

14. The Afterlife

Filling out some forms,
she is tying up loose ends –
tax claims on a ghost.

15. Migrants

From a draper's shop
in Belturbet to *No Blacks
No Irish* they came.

While she stayed at home,
he was soon their favourite
spanner in the works.

16. Ashes

They've now both returned
to their native place. England,
Ireland: it's one life.

The Fly Past

A mid-afternoon in late November,
the air chill, the sky a vacancy
when, from the corner of my eye
I sense it, a flash of sunlight
beyond my neighbour's roof
that might just be the hint
of mischief that says
he's at it again, riding his hobby horse –
the Monarchy, the Lords, Democracy,
still desperate to know what I think,
when I'm too busy to care
and it's all been said before …

And then for days, the Red Arrows
that serve no purpose and cost us money,
so why wouldn't we scrap them?
– as out of nowhere
a squadron of geese flies past
like honking virtuosi, their V
in strict alignment,
and who in seconds are gone,
having made their presence felt.

AN OPEN DRAWER

Apocryphal

My mother is always going to funerals.
She tells me that now it's all she seems to do.

Mass cards, flowers, the order of service:
'Sometimes,' she says, 'they're beautiful' –

like the old girl who filmed herself
and filled a church with smiles,

piping up in a frail contralto
'Wish me luck…'
                            then waving goodbye.

An Open Drawer

I have opened a drawer in memory,
revealing odds and ends, a treasure trove
of objects they may have thought
were useful, but mostly never were;
and laid among them the airmail letters
– light blue and flimsy.

Slicing them open with a kitchen knife
along striped edges, they eased out
the creases to read the news
from Sydney, Detroit, Toronto …
and learned how children prosper,
that work is work, and how,
wherever you travel,
you will find a face from home:

all the details of ordinary lives
translated by distances
to a gauche formality –
'Hoping, as ever, this finds you in health,'
each aspiration couched in pieties –
'One day, God willing, we will see you again.'

And buried in that drawer
with bits of twine, ribbon, forgotten keys …
the mass card for a son who died
and never made it anywhere
beyond their glistening fields,
their moist low-lying hills.

The Railway Lamp

Round and round
it went, puffing
like billy-o –
my grandparents'
novelty lamp,
bought no doubt
for them
by visiting yanks.

Like Marcel's
magic lantern
making shapes
against a wall
that conjured up
Combray,
a train is taking
me back
to Claremorris station.

It is like those
that carried
my parents, aunts
and uncles away.

Johnsforth

There is no way back
to that landscape
or the child
that you once were.

The well is boarded up;
the Iron Age fort
bulldozed flat.

They have cleared
the table.
The fire is banked.

While you were busy
elsewhere,
they switched off
the light.

Dán Deireanach

Níl aon bhealach siar
go'n tír sin
ná go'n óige
a chaith tú tráth.

Tá béal an tobair
dúnta; leagadh
an sean-ráth.

Glanta acu
atá an bord;
múchta an tine.

Agus tú cúramach
áit éigin eile,
chas siad
an solas as.

Ó Direáin
for Brian Joyce

The day I told you I'd read him,
you remembered you'd seen him once,
hunched over his pint, broodingly,
back home on Inishmore, when you

were maybe seventeen,
eighteen, or old enough at least
to get past the landlord's gaze
in that free and easy tavern

where, perched on the edge
of a swirl of talk, you listened in
to blether, blarney, *craic*,
never imagining then

your first words might fade –
though learning two trades,
you knew that one or the other
would take you away,

your eye as true as the grain
in wood or the faultless seams
you stitched for years
in Savile Row's finest suits.

And there he sat in the corner,
muttering quietly, as you observed him
watching a gull
on some weathered post.

White-throated Gull
Máirtín Ó Direáin

White-throated gull,
how well it is for you
on the back of the green swell,
its blithe ripples
lapping softly
against your breast.

White-throated gull,
change places today
that I might shake my sadness,
riding the sea,
its ripples lapping softly
against my breast.

Biscuits

In this town where I grew up, traipsing bored
to mass on Sundays, the Kingdom of God
was also founded by men who believed
in teatime treats. Abstemious fathers
of a global brand for whom the darkness
was devils that winked and slobbered in drink.

The Good News a source from which to drink
the truth, it brought hope to the weak or bored;
and those worthies knew that sloth was darkness,
obscuring the plan envisioned by God
whereby the sons must face their fathers,
building a monument to their belief.

The Tale of the Talents, so they believed,
justified their faith in money, but drink
was vice, the ruination of fathers.
The honest grafter could never be bored
and to his family might seem a god,
keeping at bay the hard times and darkness.

The tied houses were spotless. No dark nests
of vermin, no leaks occur, when belief
is practical, for then the Word of God
translates to a staunch home with food and drink.
Progress with profits inspired their Board,
a decent world for mothers and fathers

to bring up kids with a field for fathers
to kick a ball. A warm glow in darkness,
and a little sweetness when you are bored.
These were the pleasures in which they believed,
sipping contentedly anodyne drinks
of tea or coffee: potions blessed by God.

In a world where nations can pick strange gods,
collectable tins could get goods farther
than these streets I know, to regions that drink
torrential rains or, when we're in darkness,
blaze beneath a single sun. With belief
so bright and firm, I too might not be bored.

A moderate drinker, relinquishing gods,
I praise good fathers for worthy beliefs.
What they abhorred was merely the darkness.

Migrants

Rosanna Ferrario's mum and dad speak
with a funny accent. Just as yours
sound different to you because
they've come from Ireland.
Home is more than the house you live in.
They have showbands there
and do a dance called the Hucklebuck.

Dublin

Before new roads, new factories,
and ghost estates, we used to pass
through it, hiring drivers
at Westland Row to take us West
and *home*. In a land of shrines
and martyrs one chancer's
only theme was unexpected death,
quoting gory chapter and verse
at each dip and bend.

Baudelaire: Two Poems

1. Song for Autumn

We'll soon be plunged into shivering gloom.
Farewell to light and life, summer's brief reign!
The woodpile they're stacking is like a tomb
as load by load the logs crash on flagstones.

Wintry moods have taken over: their rage,
dread and loathing, their mind-numbing labour
and like the sun locked in its polar cage
my heart is frozen. My blood does not stir.

I hear with a shudder each log that falls
and thuds like a gallows slowly hammered.
My spirit's like a tower that topples
when, under siege, it's steadily battered.

Absorbing each relentless blow, I seem
to sense a coffin they're nailing somewhere.
The summer has died and now it's *autumn* –
its syllables suggesting departure.

2. The Enemy

My youth was little more than a dark storm,
lit up now and then by brilliant sunshine.
Thunder and rain have left my plot forlorn:
a few windfalls rotting, a tangled vine.

And now I have reached the autumnal phase
I will have to set to with rake and spade,
if I'm to reclaim this watery maze
through which, death-haunted, I am forced to wade.

But who's to say the flowers I yearn for
will find in soil swamped by every downpour
the mysterious blend of nutrients

growth requires, when Time is the enemy?
Feasting on the heart's blood, it drains all sense
of purpose, as signs of life slip away.

Poets' Wives
i.m. Seamus Heaney

'Away with the fairies,' my wife will say
after we've been on a walk, or I'm asked,
out of the blue, what I think of the dress
she's spotted, when I'm only vaguely there –

pursuing the rhythms inside my head
and depriving her of my attention
as slowly, mysteriously, the lines
coalesce into 'another damn poem'.

And if at times I frustrate her, the fault
must lie with you whose work first inspired me,
devouring your books, until each three- four-
or five-year interval has marked my life

from its adolescence: segments of time
that once dragged, yet speed exponentially
now that I see behind me fallow years
of paid work, bills, responsibility;

thankful at least for the late revival
of a gift which – however slight – I know
I betrayed: a bind that your exemplar,
Yeats, defined and you surely understood

when, in 'An Afterwards', perhaps only
half-jokingly, you had Marie plunge you,
and all your kind, into the ninth circle
for such assiduous care of the word.

Lines for a Fighter
i.m. Muhammad Ali

Before abandoning the name
their masters gave your fathers
you were just some *colored* kid,
segregated and sanctified
in the Church of Hallelujahs,
holding your own on streets
where Cassius Clay was what
they called you, stamped
and seared by a slaver's brand.

The voice of conscience
was Emmett Till, the imaginary
twin whose date of birth
obsessed you, his features lying
like bruised fruit
in the bigots' torchlight –
an omen for the uppity.

For you outraged them too
with your lip and fancy footwork,
your Five Pillars of Islam.
Turning up the heat with verses,
you out-rhymed no-hopers.

Pilgrims
for Ziyad, Tamim & Rafiq

When the day has come,
you will make a journey
to the city of Mecca.

Each of you a pilgrim
dressed in white,
you will cast the stones

that set you free
from Shaitaan, the evil one.
Circling the Ka'aba

you will feel around you
the crowd surging
like a river in spate;

and though it's a distance
I cannot travel,
the scallop shells

on my school badge
made me a pilgrim too,
like those who had tramped

to the far-flung shrine
of Santiago
de Compostela.

Caversham Revisited

I thought time had made me a stranger
to kin I've accompanied here
and souls whose terminal progress
filled mornings free from school;
yet now with those remaining
and some who've since appeared
I feel again a shared unease –
returning this morning,
for the first time in years,
to where my mother's loitering
on the brink of her sister's grave;
and the battered CD player,
laid on grass, pours forth
its thin lament, in spite of drizzle,
impenetrable cloud,
and the plates of food calling,
over which we'll swap email addresses
and catch up with news,
while an octogenarian aunt insists
I haven't changed one bit
from when I was six or seven.

Requiescant

There at its lower end that screen of trees,
still bare, defines its peaceable limits,
a pause in the city's din –
the purposes and rush of the living
locked in distant streets.

Acknowledgements

I take the opportunity to thank the editors of the following journals and websites where some of these poems or earlier versions of them first appeared: *Agenda, Amaryllis, Black Light Engine Room, Cannon's Mouth, Clear Poetry, The Cortland Review* (USA), *Cyphers, Dream Catcher, Eyewear, The Frogmore Papers, The Galway Review, Ink Sweat & Tears, The High Window, I am not a Silent Poet, The Interpreter's House, The Irish Literary Review, The Journal, The Lake, London Grip, Message in a Bottle, Nutshells & Nuggets, The Ofi Press Magazine* (Mexico), *Pennine Platform, Poetry Salzburg Review, The Poets' Republic, The Screech Owl, Seventh Quarry, Stachtes* (Greece), *The Wilderness House Review* (USA), and *Yareah* (USA).

Some were also published in the following anthologies: *The Book of Love and Loss* (edited by R.V. Bailey and June Hall for The Belgrave Press 2014), *Poets in Person* (edited by Aprilia Zank for Indigo Dreams 2014) and *This Quiet Spot, The Reading University Creative Arts Anthology 2013*.

I would also like to express my heartfelt thanks to William Bedford, Ian House, Kevin Mulqueen and Wendy Klein for their invaluable scrutiny of the final text.

Several poems in the opening section were inspired by the work of the French photographer Willi Ronis (1910 – 2009): 'Le Petit Parisien, 1952', 'Chez Maxe, Joinville, 1947', 'Le Nu Provençal', 'The Lovers at the Bastille', 'Mill Girl', 'Photographer'.

'Dán Deireannach', the Irish language version of 'Johnsforth', was translated anonymously, and supplied by the good offices of Aifric Mac Aodha. Finally, for those interested in such matters, the mystery bird in 'Ornithology' was eventually identified as *Coragyps atratus*.

Cultured Llama Publishing
Poems | Stories | Curious Things

Cultured Llama was born in a converted stable. This creature of humble birth drank greedily from the creative source of the poets, writers, artists and musicians that visited, and soon the llama fulfilled the destiny of its given name.

Cultured Llama aspires to quality from the first creative thought through to the finished product.

www.culturedllama.co.uk

Also published by Cultured Llama

Poetry

strange fruits by Maria C. McCarthy
Paperback; 72pp; 203×127mm; 978-0-9568921-0-2; July 2011

A Radiance by Bethany W. Pope
Paperback; 70pp; 203×127mm; 978-0-9568921-3-3; June 2012

The Strangest Thankyou by Richard Thomas
Paperback; 98pp; 203×127mm; 978-0-9568921-5-7; November 2012

The Night My Sister Went to Hollywood by Hilda Sheehan
Paperback; 82pp; 203×127mm; 978-0-9568921-8-8; March 2013

Notes from a Bright Field by Rose Cook
Paperback; 104pp; 203×127mm; 978-0-9568921-9-5; July 2013

Sounds of the Real World by Gordon Meade
Paperback; 104pp; 203×127mm; 978-0-9926485-0-3; August 2013

The Fire in Me Now by Michael Curtis
Paperback; 90pp; 203×127mm; 978-0-9926485-4-1; August 2014

Short of Breath by Vivien Jones
Paperback; 102pp; 203×127mm; 978-0-9926485-5-8; October 2014

Cold Light of Morning by Julian Colton
Paperback; 90pp; 203×127mm; 978-0-9926485-7-2; March 2015

Automatic Writing by John Brewster
Paperback; 96pp; 203×127mm; 978-0-9926485-8-9; July 2015

Zygote Poems by Richard Thomas
Paperback; 66pp; 178×127mm; 978-0-9932119-5-9; July 2015

Les Animots: A Human Bestiary by Gordon Meade, images by Douglas Robertson
Hardback; 166pp; 203×127mm; 978-0-9926485-9-6; December 2015

Memorandum: Poems for the Fallen by Vanessa Gebbie
Paperback; 90pp; 203×127mm; 978-0-9932119-4-2; February 2016

The Light Box by Rosie Jackson
Paperback; 108pp; 203×127mm; 978-0-9932119-7-3; March 2016

There Are No Foreign Lands by Mark Holihan
Paperback; 96pp; 203×127mm; 978-0-9932119-8-0; June 2016

Short stories

Canterbury Tales on a Cockcrow Morning by Maggie Harris
Paperback; 138pp; 203×127mm; 978-0-9568921-6-4; September 2012

As Long as it Takes by Maria C. McCarthy
Paperback; 168pp; 203×127mm; 978-0-9926485-1-0; February 2014

In Margate by Lunchtime by Maggie Harris
Paperback; 204pp; 203×127mm; 978-0-9926485-3-4; February 2015

The Lost of Syros by Emma Timpany
Paperback; 128pp; 203×127mm; 978-0-9932119-2-8; July 2015

Only the Visible Can Vanish by Anna Maconochie
Paperback; 158pp; 203×127mm; 978-0-9932119-9-7; September 2016

Who Killed Emil Kreisler? by Nigel Jarrett
Paperback; 208pp; 203×127mm; 978-0-9568921-1-9; November 2016

A Short History of Synchronised Breathing and other stories by
Vanessa Gebbie
Paperback; 132pp; 203×127mm; 978-0-9568921-2-6; February 2017

Curious things

**Digging Up Paradise: Potatoes, People and Poetry in the Garden of
England** by Sarah Salway
Paperback; 164pp; 203×203mm; 978-0-9926485-6-5; June 2014

**Punk Rock People Management: A No-Nonsense Guide to Hiring,
Inspiring and Firing Staff** by Peter Cook
Paperback; 40pp; 210×148mm; 978-0-9932119-0-4; February 2015

Do it Yourself: A History of Music in Medway by Stephen H. Morris
Paperback; 504pp; 229×152mm; 978-0-9926485-2-7; April 2015

The Music of Business: Business Excellence Fused with Music by
Peter Cook – NEW EDITION
Paperback; 318pp; 210×148mm; 978-0-9932119-1-1; May 2015

The Hungry Writer by Lynne Rees
Paperback; 246pp; 244×170mm; 978-0-9932119-3-5; September 2015

The Ecology of Everyday Things by Mark Everard
Hardback; 126pp; 216×140mm; 978-0-9932119-6-6; November 2015

Lightning Source UK Ltd.
Milton Keynes UK
UKHW01f0626230618
324656UK00001B/92/P